The Olden Time Series - Volume V

HENRY MASON BROOKS

1886

TABLE OF CONTENTS

SOME STRANGE AND CURIOUS PUNISHMENTS
OLD NEW ENGLAND

SOME STRANGE AND CURIOUS PUNISHMENTS

In the month of January, 1761, "Joseph Bennett, John Jenkins, Owen McCarty, and John Wright were publickly whipt at the Cart's Tail thro' the City of New York for petty Larceny,"—so the newspaper account states,— "pursuant to Sentence inflicted on them by the Court of Quarter Sessions held last Week for the Trial of Robbers," etc. In March the same year "One Andrew Cayto received 49 Stripes at the public Whipping Post" in Boston "for House-robbing; viz., 39 for robbing one House, and 10 for robbing another." In 1762 "Jeremiah Dexter, of Walpole, pursuant to Sentence, stood in the Pillory in that Town the space of one Hour for uttering two Counterfeit Mill'd Dollars, knowing them to be such." At Ipswich, Mass., June 16, 1763, "one Francis Brown, for stealing a large quantity of Goods, was found Guilty, and it being the second Conviction, he was sentenced by the Court to sit on the Gallows an Hour with a Rope about his Neck, to be whipt 30 Stripes, and pay treble Damages. He says he was born in Lisbon, and has been a great Thief."

We extract the following from the "Boston Chronicle," Nov. 20, 1769:—

We hear from Worcester that on the eighth instant one Lindsay stood in the Pillory there one hour, after which he received 30 stripes at the public whipping post, and was then branded in the hand; his crime was forgery.

Lindsay was probably branded with the letter F, by means of a hot iron, on the palm of his right hand; this was the custom in such cases.

In Boston, in June, 1762, "the noted Dr. Seth Hudson and Joshua How stood a second Time in the Pillory for the space of one Hour, and the former received 20 and the latter 39 Stripes." In the same town in February, 1764, "one David Powers for Stealing was sentenced to be whip't 20

Stripes, to pay tripel Damages, being £30, and Costs. And one John Gray, Cordwainer, for endeavouring to spread the Infection of the Small Pox, was sentenced to pay a Fine of £6, to suffer three months' Imprisonment, and to pay Costs." In New York in January, 1767, "A Negro Wench was executed for stealing sundry Articles out of the House of Mr. Forbes; and one John Douglass was burnt in the Hand for Stealing a Copper Kettle." In the last half of the eighteenth century it appears to have been a capital crime for negroes to steal. At Springfield, Mass., in October, 1767, "one Elnathan Muggin was found Guilty of passing Counterfeit Dollars, and sentenced to have his Ears cropped," etc. On reading these quaint accounts we are led to inquire whether the punishment for crime in "olden times" was more severe than at the present time. Many people think it was, and justly so, and argue that crime has consequently greatly increased of late years, on account of the lightness of modern sentences or the uncertainty about punishment. This may be true. Crime is said to increase with population always. According to Mr. Buckle, it can be calculated with a considerable degree of accuracy. We can estimate, for instance, the probable number of murders which will take place in a year in a given number of inhabitants. Whether this theory is true or not would require a vast amount of study and observation to determine. We know that population in our time crowds in cities; especially is this true of the classes most likely to furnish criminals. Still, in spite of this, do not most of us feel that it has of late years been rather safer to reside in a city than in the country? Consider the numbers of lawless and too often cruel tramps which have overrun the country towns and villages for a few years past, making it so unsafe for women to walk unattended in woods and highways, even in the quietest parts of New England, where once they could go with perfect safety alone and at all hours. No laws can be too severe against cruel tramps. It has been affirmed that people who live in cities are in reality more moral than country people of the same class.

Is this state of things brought about by the infliction of light sentences, or is it caused by the increase among us of a bad foreign element? We have heard many serious and humane persons express themselves as in favor of a restoration of the whipping-post and stocks, really supposing that these things would lessen crime. But is it likely that the old methods of punishment would be considered by criminals themselves as severer than the present? Let us see what some of the last century rogues thought about the matter. At a session of the Supreme Judicial Court held at Salem, Mass., in December, 1788, one James Ray was sentenced, for stealing goods from the shop of Captain John Hathorne (a relative of Nathaniel Hawthorne), to sit upon the gallows with a rope about his neck for an hour, to be whipped with thirty-nine stripes, and to be confined to hard labor on Castle Island (Boston Harbor) for three years. "It is observable of this man," the account continues, "that he has been lately released from a two years' service at the Castle, that during the trial he was very merry and impudent, and continued in the same humor while his sentence was reading, holding up his head and looking boldly at the Court, till the three years' confinement was mentioned; when his countenance changed, his head dropped on his breast, and he fetched a deep groan,—an instance of how much more dreadful the idea of labor is to such villains than that of Corporal punishment."

At a session of the Court of Oyer and Terminer held at Norristown, Pa., for the county of Montgomery, Oct. 11, 1786, we are furnished with a case in point. "A bill was presented against Philip Hoosnagle for burglary, who was convicted by the traverse Jury on the clearest testimony. He was, after a very pathetick and instructing admonition from the bench, sentenced to five years' hard labour, under the new act of Assembly. It was with some difficulty that this reprobate was prevailed upon to make the election of labour instead of the halter, ... a convincing proof," the report says, "that the punishments directed by the new law are more terrifying to idle vagabonds than all the horrors of an ignominious death."

Probably there are many more cases on record where criminals preferred death to imprisonment. Burglary and forgery were once punished by death. We have all noticed on the old Continental currency these words: "Death to counterfeit this."

On the 17th June, 1791, Samuel Cook, in the eighty-fourth year of his age, was executed at Johnstown, N.Y., for forgery. On the 6th December, 1787, William Clarke was executed at Northampton for burglary; the same day Charles Rose and Jonathan Bly were executed at Lenox for robbery. On the 4th May, 1786, at Worcester, Johnson Green, indicted for three burglaries committed in one night within the space of about half a mile, was tried on one indictment, convicted, and received sentence of death. The papers contain numerous similar cases. It would be useless to enumerate them all; we give only a few in order to show what the punishment formerly awarded to these crimes really was. We do not, of course, know the circumstances attending all these cases; but robbery and burglary are usually premeditated, and the criminals are prepared to commit murder if it should be necessary for their purpose, so that we can have no sympathy with the perpetrators. Our sympathy ought, we think, to go to the victims.

OLD NEW ENGLAND

Early in the settlement of New England, as is pretty generally known, some of the laws and punishments were singular enough. A few extracts from Felt's "Annals of Salem" may not be out of place here, as illustrating our subject:—

"In 1637, Dorothy Talby, for beating her husband, is ordered to be bound and chained to a post."

"In 1638, the Assistants order two Salem men to sit in the Stocks, on Lecture day, for travelling on the Sabbath."

"In 1644, Mary, wife of Thomas Oliver, was sentenced to be publickly whipped for reproaching the Magistrates."

"In August, 1646, for slandering the Elders, she had a cleft stick put on her tongue for half an hour." Felt says: "It is evident that her standing out for what she considered 'woman's rights' brought her into frequent and severe trouble. Mr. Winthrop says that she excelled Mrs. Hutchinson in zeal and eloquence."

She finally, in 1650, left the colony, after having caused much trouble to the Church and the authorities.

"In 1649, women were prosecuted in Salem for scolding," and probably in many cases whipped or ducked.

"May 15, 1672, the General Court of Massachusetts orders that Scolds and Railers shall be gagged or set in a ducking-stool and dipped over head and ears three times."

This treatment we should suppose would be likely to make the victims very pleasant, especially in cold weather.

"May 3, 1669, Thomas Maule is ordered to be whipped for saying that Mr. Higginson preached lies, and that his instruction was 'the doctrine of devils.'"

Josiah Southwick, Mrs. Wilson, Mrs. Buffum, and others, Quakers, for making disturbances in the meeting-house, etc., were whipped at the cart's tail through the town. Southwick, for returning after having been banished, was whipped through the towns of Boston, Roxbury, and Dedham. These are only a few of the cases of the punishments inflicted upon the Quakers. Mr. Felt says in reference to the persecution of the Quakers:

"Before any new denomination becomes consolidated, some of its members are apt to show more zeal than discretion. No sect who are regular and useful should have an ill name for the improprieties committed by a few of them."

Our "pious forefathers," we must confess, were too apt to be a little hard towards those who annoyed them with their tongue and pen upon Church doctrine and discipline or the administration of the government. As early as 1631, one Philip Ratclif is sentenced by the Assistants to pay £40, to be whipped, to have his ears cropped, and to be banished. What had he done to merit such a punishment as this? He had made "hard speeches against Salem Church, as well as the Government." "The execution of this decision," Mr. Felt says, "was represented in England to the great disadvantage of Massachusetts." Jeffries was not yet on the bench in England.

In 1652 a man was fined for excess of apparel "in bootes, rebonds, gould and silver lace."

Mr. Charles W. Palfrey contributed in 1866 to the "Salem Register" the following interesting item on the Salem witchcraft trials:

Among the many attempts to remedy the mischiefs caused by the witchcraft delusion, the subjoined is not without interest. About eighteen years after the memorable year, 1692, four members, a committee of the Legislature, were sent to Salem to hear certain parties and receive certain petitions, and the following is the record, in the Journal, of their Report:—

October 26, 1711. Present in Council, His Excellency Joseph Dudley, Esqr., Governor, John Hathorne, Samuel Sewall, Jonathan Corwin, Joseph Lynde, Penn Townsend, John Higginson, Daniel Epes, Andrew Belcher, etc., etc.

Report of the Committee appointed, Relating to the Affair of Witchcraft in the year 1692; viz.—

We whose Names are subscribed in Obedience to your Honours' Act at a Court held the last of May, 1710, for our inserting the Names of the several Persons who were condemned for Witchcraft in the year 1692, and of the Damages they sustained by their prosecution; Being met at Salem, for the Ends aforesaid, the 13th Septem., 1710, Upon Examination of the Records of the several Persons condemned, Humbly offer to your Honours the Names as follows, to be inserted for the Reversing their Attainders: Elizabeth How, George Jacob, Mary Easty, Mary Parker, Mr. George Burroughs, Gyles Cory and Wife, Rebecca Nurse, John Willard, Sarah Good, Martha Carrier, Samuel Wardel, John Procter, Sarah Wild, Mary

Bradbury, Abigail Falkner, Abigail Hobbs, Ann Foster, Rebecca Eams, Dorcas Hoar, Mary Post, Mary Lacy:

And having heard the several Demands of the Damages of the aforesaid Persons and those in their behalf; and upon Conference have so moderated their respective Demands that We doubt not but they will be readily complied with by your Honours.

Which respective Demands are as follows:—

Elizabeth How, Twelve Pounds; George Jacob, Seventy nine Pounds; Mary Easty, Twenty Pounds; Mary Parker, Eight Pounds; Mr. George Burroughs, Fifty Pounds; Gyles Core and Martha Core his Wife, Twenty one Pounds; Rebecca Nurse, Twenty five Pounds; John Willard, Twenty Pounds; Sarah Good, Thirty Pounds; Martha Carrier, Seven Pounds six shillings; Samuel Wardell and Sarah his Wife, Thirty six Pounds fifteen shillings; John Proctor and —— Proctor his Wife, One Hundred and fifty Pounds; Sarah Wilde, Fourteen Pounds; Mrs. Mary Bradbury, Twenty Pounds; Abigail Faulkner, Twenty Pounds; Abigail Hobbs, Ten Pounds; Ann Foster, Six Pounds ten shillings; Rebecca Eams, Ten Pounds; Dorcas Hoar, Twenty one Pounds seventeen shillings; Mary Post Eight Pounds fourteen shillings; Mary Lacey Eight Pounds ten shillings. The Whole amounting unto Five Hundred and seventy eight Pounds, and twelve shillings.

(Sign'd) Jno. Appleton, Thomas Noyes, John Burrill, Nehem'a Jewett.

Salem, Septemr. 14, 1711.

Read and Accepted in the House of Represent'ves

Signed JOHN BURRILL Speak'r

Read and Concur'd in Council

Consented to   J. DUDLEY.

The following quaint memorandum of the expenses of the commission is minuted in the report, viz.:—

Ye Acct of gr servts

Charges 3 days a peis ourselves and horses 4.0.0.

Entertainment at Salem Mr. Pratts 1.3.0.

Major Sewals attendans and sendg notifications

to all Concerned 1.0.0.

£6.3.0.

It is a grave error into which many modern writers have been drawn, when alluding to Salem witchcraft, to lay the responsibility of that dire delusion entirely upon Salem people, as if they alone were to be held accountable for the dreadful occurrences of 1692. The laws of England in those days, all the authorities of New England, and, with but rare exceptions, all the people everywhere throughout the civilized world, recognized witchcraft as a fact and believed it to be a crime. The most learned men in England and in other countries believed fully in witchcraft. Sir Matthew Hale had given a legal opinion on the subject; Lord Bacon believed in witchcraft; and there are strong reasons for thinking that Shakspeare and other great men of the time of Queen Elizabeth and still later believed in it fully. Cotton Mather, Judge Sewall, Peter Sargent, Lieutenant-Governor Stoughton, all belonging to Boston, were the leaders in the proceedings against the witches of 1692.

HUNG IN CHAINS.

In the papers that we have examined we have not found any instances recorded of the old English law of hanging the remains of executed criminals in chains as having been carried into effect in our country. But from some investigations of Mr. James E. Mauran, of Newport, R.I., we learn that on March 12, 1715, one Mecum of that town was executed for murder and his body was hung in chains on Miantonomy Hill, where the remains of an Indian were then hanging, who had been executed Sept. 12, 1712. Mecum was a Scotchman, and lived at the head of Broad Street. A negro was hanged in Newport in 1679, and his remains were exposed on the same hill.

A BOOK ORDERED TO BE BURNED BY THE COUNCIL IN 1695.

The "Salem Observer" of Feb. 14, 1829, quotes from the Rev. Dr. Bentley's "Diary" as follows:—

Tho's Maule, shopkeeper of Salem, is brought before the Council to answer for his printing and publishing a pamphlet of 260 pages, entitled "Truth held forth and maintained," owns the book but will not own all, till he sees his copy which is at New-York with Bradford, who printed it. Saith he writt to ye Gov'r of N. York before he could get it printed. Book is ordered to be burnt—being stuff'd with notorious lyes and scandals, and he recognizes to answer it next Court of Assize and gen'l gaol delivery to be held for the County of Essex. He acknowledges that what was written concerning the circumstance of Major Gen. Atherton's death was a mistake (p. 112 and 113), was chiefly insisted on against him, which I believe was a surprize to him, he expecting to be examined in some point of religion, as should seem by his bringing his bible under his arm.

Thomas Maule was a Quaker who lived in Essex Street, Salem, on the spot now occupied by James B. Curwen, Esq., as a residence.

Imported books were ordered to be burned in Boston as early as 1653, by command of the General Court; but we believe this is the first instance of burning an American book.

Punishment for wearing long hair in New England. From an old Salem paper.

Puritanical Zeal. It is known that there was one of the statutes in our ancestors' code which imposed a penalty for the wearing of long hair. At the time Endicott was the magistrate of this town he caused the following order to be passed:—

"John Gatshell is fyened ten shillings for building upon the town's ground without leave; and in case he shall cutt of his loung hair of his head in to sevill frame (fewell flame?) in the meane time, shall have abated five shillings his fine, to be paid in to the Towne meeting within two months from this time, and have leave to go in his building in the meantime."

Purchas says of long hair that—

"It is an ornament to the female sex, a token of subjection, an ensign of modesty; but modesty grows short in men as their hair grows long, and a neat perfumed, frizled, pouldered bush hangs but as a token,—vini non vendibilis, of much wine, little wit, of men weary of manhood, of civility, of christianity, which would faine turn (as the least doe imitate) American salvages, infidels, barbarians, or women at the least and best."

Prynne, who wrote in 1632, considers men who nourish their hair like women, as an abomination to the Lord, and says—

"No wonder that the wearing of long haire should make men abominable unto God himselfe, since it was an abomination even among heathen men. Witnesse the examples of Heliogabalus, Sardanapalus, Nero, Sporus, Caius Caligula, and others."

He refers to the opinions of the fathers and the decrees of the Old Councils to prove that—

"Long hair and love locks are bushes of vanity whereby the Devil leads and holds men captive."

In a Boston paper, Aug. 11, 1789, we find the following ludicrous account of the unfaithfulness of an officer in the duty of whipping a culprit:—

On Thursday, 11 culprits received the discipline of the post in this town. The person obtained by the High Sheriff to inflict the punishment, from sympathetick feeling for his brother culprits, was very tender in dealing out his strokes, and not adding weight to them, although repeatedly ordered; the Sheriff, to his honour, took the whip from his hand, by an application of it to his shoulders drove him from the stage, and with the assistance of his Deputies inflicted the punishment of the law on all the culprits. The citizens who were assembled, complimented the Sheriff with three cheers for the manly, determined manner in which he executed his duty.

In the "Boston Courier," September, 1825, is an account of the conviction of a common drunkard at the age of 103! It seems hardly possible that such a case could have occurred, and in New England, too. This item is copied from the "Salem Observer." If it is true, it can hardly be said that the man shortened his days by the use of liquor. They had, however, good, pure rum in those days.

Police Court. Donald McDonald, a Scotchman reported to be one hundred and three years of age, was brought before the court yesterday charged with being a common drunkard, of which he had been convicted once before. Donald stated that he had been in various battles of the Revolution, had sailed with Paul Jones, and was at the taking of Quebec. He was found guilty and sentenced to the House of Correction for three months.

Donald M'Donald, the Scotchman, who has numbered upwards of 110 years, was sent to the House of Industry on Saturday of last week, in a state of intoxication. He had been suffered to go at large but four days previous, and during two of them was seen about our streets a drunken brawler.—Boston Patriot, 1829.

NEW ENGLAND IN 1686.

John Dunton, writing from Boston in 1686 to his friends in England, quotes some of the Province laws then in force. He says:—

For being drunk they either Whip or impose a Fine of Five shillings; And yet, notwithstanding this Law, there are several of them so addicted to it that they begin to doubt whether it be a Sin or no, and seldom go to Bed without Muddy Brains.

For Cursing and Swearing they bore through the Tongue with a hot Iron.

For kissing a woman in the Street, though but in way of Civil Salute, Whipping or a Fine (Their way of Whipping Criminals is by Tying them to a Gun at the Town House, and when so Ty'd whipping them at the pleasure of the Magistrate and according to the Nature of the Offence).

For Adultery they are put to Death, and so for Witchcraft, For that, there are a great many Witches in this Country andc.

Scolds they gag and set them at their own Doors, for certain hours together for all comers and goers to gaze at. Were this a Law in England and well Executed it wou'd in a little Time prove an Effectual Remedy to cure the Noise that is in many Women's heads.

Stealing is punished with Restoring four-fold if able; if not, they are sold for some years, and so are poor Debtors. I have not heard of many Criminals of this sort. But for Lying and Cheating they out-vye Judas and all the false other cheats in Hell. Nay, they make a Sport of it: Looking upon Cheating as a commendable Piece of Ingenuity, commending him that has the most skill to commit a piece of Roguery; which in their Dialect (like those of our Yea-and-Nay-Friends in England) they call by the genteel Name of Out-Witting a Man and won't own it to be cheating.

After mentioning the case of a man in Boston who bought a horse of a countryman who could not read and gave him a note payable at the "Day of the Resurrection," etc. Dunton goes on to say: "In short, These Bostonians enrich themselves by the ruine of Strangers, etc.... But all these things pass under the Notion of Self-Preservation and Christian Policy."

It would hardly be fair to quote all this from Dunton's letters unless we added what he says of Boston in another place; namely, "And though the Generality are what I have described them, yet is there as sincere a Pious and truly Religious People among them as is any where in the Whole World to be found."

It seems to have been quite common at one time to sell prisoners. At the Supreme Judicial Court in Salem, in November, 1787, "Elizabeth Leathe of

Lynn, for harbouring thieves and receiving stolen goods, was convicted and sentenced to be whipped twenty stripes and to be sold for six months." Also at a session of the same Court, held in Boston in September, 1791, six persons were convicted of theft and sentenced to be whipped and pay costs, or to be sold for periods of from six months to four years. At this same Court one Seth Johnson appears to have received what seems to us a rather severe sentence, although of course we do not know all the circumstances of the case. He was convicted of theft on three indictments and was sentenced to be "whipt 65 stripes and confined to hard labor for nine years." The Court at Salem, before referred to, passed on one Catharine Derby a very heavy sentence for stealing from Captain Hathorne's shop. It was, "To sit upon the gallows one hour with a rope about her neck, to be whipped 20 stripes, pay £14 to Capt. Hathorne, and costs of prosecution." This is almost as bad as the old saying, "being hung and paying forty shillings."

This practice of selling convicts was nothing more or less than making slaves of them,—for a limited period, of course; but perhaps it was in many instances a punishment more to be desired by the victims than being confined in prison, especially if they were well treated. The prisons in those days had not "modern conveniences," and probably in some cases were hardly decent. The condition of the jail in Portsmouth, N.H., in February, 1789, is thus described by a prisoner who made his escape from there by digging through the chimney. His account is interesting in this connection. The paper from which we take it says: "But for fear his quitting his lodgings in so abrupt a manner might lay him open to censure, he wrote the following on the wall:—

"The reason of my going is because I have no fire to comfort myself with, and very little provision. So I am sure, if I was to stay any longer I should perish to death. Look at that bed there! Do you think it fit for any person to lie on?

"If you are well, I am well;
Mend the chimney, and all's well!

"To the gentlemen and officers of Portsmouth from your humble servant, "William Fall.

"N.B. I am very sorry that I did not think of this before, for if I had, your people should not have had the pleasure of seeing me take the lashes."

The whipping-post and stocks were discontinued in Massachusetts early in the present century. On the 15th of January, 1801, one Hawkins stood an hour in the pillory in Court Street (now Washington Street), Salem, and had his ear cropped for the crime of forgery, pursuant to the sentence of the Supreme Court.

It would be easy to multiply cases showing the old methods of dealing with criminals; but we think we have cited enough for our readers to be able to form some judgment as to the desirability of reviving the old and degrading systems, even if it could be done. It does seem sometimes that there are brutes in the shape of men whose cruelty, especially in the case of crimes against women, makes them deserving of the worst punishment that could be inflicted for the protection of society; but for the general run of such comparatively light offences as petty larceny, etc., beating and branding with hot irons must be considered barbarous in the extreme, and more after the manner of savages than Christians. We always thought that the beating of scholars—a practice once very common in schools—for such trifling offences as whispering and looking off the book, was a gross outrage, and the parent knowing and allowing it was in our opinion as guilty as the schoolmaster. Of course we will not deny that teachers did, then as now, have a great deal to put up with from saucy, "good-for-nothing" boys, to whom the rod could not well be spared; but we do not allude to such cases. We knew a master whose delight, apparently, was pounding and beating little boys,—he did not touch the large ones. And yet he was generally considered a first-rate teacher. Parents upheld him in anything he chose to do with the boys, and if they complained at home, they were told that it must have been their fault to be punished at all. This man every morning took the Bible in one hand and his rattan in the other and walked backward and forward on the floor in front of the desks while the boys read aloud, each boy reading two or three verses; and woe be to any boy who made a mistake, such as mispronouncing a word! Although he might never have been instructed as to its pronunciation, he was at once pounded on the head or rapped over the knuckles. Of course he never forgot that particular word. And this teacher was called only "strict"! If ever a man deserved the pillory, it was that teacher.

Possibly some of our readers may think that there is another side to this story; for the benefit of such we give some lines from the "Salem Gazette," Feb. 6, 1824.

From the Connecticut Centinel.

THE SCHOOLMASTER'S SOLILOQUY.

To whip, or not to whip?—that is the question.
Whether 'tis easier in the mind to suffer
The deaf'ning clamor of some fifty urchins,
Or take birch and ferule 'gainst the rebels,
And by opposing end it? To whip—to flog—
Each day, and by a whip to say we end
The whispering, shuffling, and ceaseless buzzing
Which a school is heir to—'tis a consummation
Devoutly to be wished. To whip, to flog,
To whip, and not reform—aye, there's the rub.
For by severity what ills may come,

When we've dismissed and to our lodging gone,
Must give us pain. There's the respect
That makes the patience of a teacher's life.
For who would bear the thousand plagues of a school,—
The girlish giggle, the tyro's awkwardness,
The pigmy pedant's vanity, the mischief,
The sneer, the laugh, the pouting insolence,
With all the hum-drum clatter of a school,
When he himself might his quietus make
With a bare hickory? Who would willing bear
To groan and sweat under a noisy life,
But that the dread of something after school
(That hour of rumor, from whose slanderous tongue
Few Tutors e'er are free) puzzles the will,
And makes us rather bear these lesser ills,
Than fly to those of greater magnitude.
Thus error does make cowards of us all;
And thus the native hue of resolution
Is sicklied over with undue clemency,
And pedagogues of great pith and spirit,
With this regard their firmness turn away,
And lose the name of government.

We here record a curious affair which took place in the State of Georgia in the year 1811. At the Superior Court at Milledgeville a Mrs. Palmer, who, the account states, "seems to have been rather glib of the tongue, was indicted, tried, convicted, and, in pursuance of the sentence of the Court, was punished by being publicly ducked in the Oconee River for—scolding." This, we are told, was the first instance of the kind that had ever occurred in that State, and "numerous spectators attended the execution of the sentence." A paper copying this account says that the "crime is old, but the punishment is new," and that "in the good old days of our Ancestors, when an unfortunate woman was accused of Witchcraft she was tied neck and heels and thrown into a pond of Water: if she drowned, it was agreed that she was no witch; if she swam, she was immediately tied to a stake and burnt alive. But who ever heard that our pious ancestors ducked women for scolding?" This writer is much mistaken; for it is well known that in England (and perhaps in this country in early times) the "ducking-stool" was resorted to for punishing "scolds." This was before the days of "women's rights," for there is no record of any man having been punished in this way.

It is said that the ducking-stool was used in Virginia at one time. Thomas Hartley writes from there to Governor Endicott of Massachusetts in 1634, giving an account of the punishing a woman "who by the violence of her tongue had made her house and neighborhood uncomfortable." She was ducked five times before she repented; "then cried piteously, 'Let me go! let me go! by God's help I'll sin so no more.' They then drew back ye Machine, untied ye Ropes, and let her walk home in her wetted Clothes a hopefully penitent woman." In the "American Historical Record," vol. i., will be found a very interesting account of this singular affair, with an engraving of the "ducking-stool." Bishop Meade, in his "Old Churches," etc., says there was a law in Virginia against scolds and slanderers, and gives an instance of a woman ordered to be ducked three times from a vessel lying in James River. There must have been very severe practices in Virginia in the early days, according to Bishop Meade. We refer persons especially interested in this subject to Hone's "Day Book and Table Book," or Chambers's "Book of Days," both English publications, for a full account of the ducking-stool and scold's bridle, formerly used in England for the punishment of scolding women. It is not pleasant to think that such a shameful practice was ever resorted to, but it appears to be well authenticated. We cannot, however, read English history, or any other history, without finding a vast number of disagreeable facts which we are obliged to believe. Some things, too, have occurred in our own country that we should like to forget.

All over the country we are nowadays troubled with "strikes." Such "irregularities" must have been treated in a different spirit half a century ago from what they are now. In these days the "strikers" attempt to dictate terms, and in some cases succeed; although as a general thing they get the worst of the struggle. The method of dealing with such matters fifty years ago is briefly set forth in the "Salem Observer," March 29, 1829. It says: "Turn-out in New York. There has been a turn-out for higher wages among the laborers in the city of New York. Several of the ring-leaders have been arrested and ordered to give heavy bonds for their appearance at Court." In September, 1827, some sailors struck in Boston for higher wages, formed a procession, and marched through the city, making considerable noise with their cheers, etc. They issued the following proclamation, which was read by the leader now and then, and responded to with loud cheers: "Attention! We, the blue Jackets now in the city of Boston, agree that we will not ship for less than $15 a month, and that we will punish any one who shall ship for less in such way as we think proper, and strip the vessel [which he ships in]. What say you?" At the Common they were met by a militia company, who charged upon them; some men of both sides were knocked down, but no lives were lost or blood shed. In the afternoon the sailors were out again with drum and fife. The paper from which we obtain this information says that they probably would not get any advance, as it is assured by a shipper that he found no difficulty in procuring crews at the customary wages. Probably it was not intended that the military should do more than endeavor to keep order.

It is rather surprising that there should have been no conviction for felony in the County of Essex from 1692, when the witches were tried, until 1771,—a period of seventy-nine years. It would so appear, however, from the following extract from the "Essex Gazette," Nov. 12, 1771:—

Last Wednesday Morning the Trial of Bryan Sheehen for committing a Rape on the Body of Mrs. Abial Hollowell, Wife of Mr. Benjamin Hollowell, of Marblehead, in September last, came on before the Superior Court of Judicature, at the Court-House in this Town. The Trial lasted from between nine and ten o'Clock A.M. till three in the Afternoon, when the Jury withdrew, and in about one Hour brought in their Verdict, GUILTY. Mrs. Hollowell's Testimony against the Prisoner was fully corroborated by the Physician who attended her, and by the People who were in the House, at and after the Perpetration of the Crime; by which the Guilt and Barbarity of the Prisoner was so fully demonstrated, that the Verdict of the Jury has given universal Satisfaction.

This Bryan Sheehen (who has not yet received his Sentence) is the first Person, as far as we can learn, that has been convicted of Felony, in this large County, since the memorable Year 1692, commonly called Witch-Time.

From the "Boston Post-Boy," February, 1763.

BOSTON, January 31.

At the Superiour Court held at Charlestown last Week, Samuel Bacon of Bedford, and Meriam Fitch, Wife of Benjamin Fitch of said Bedford, were convicted of being notorious Cheats, and of having by Fraud, Craft and Deceit, possess'd themselves of Fifteen Hundred Johannes, the property of a third Person; were Sentenced to be each of them set in the Pillory one Hour, with a Paper on each of their Breasts with the Words a CHEAT wrote in Capitals thereon, to suffer three Months Imprisonment, and to be bound to their good Behaviour for one Year, and to pay Costs.

From the "Massachusetts Gazette," May 1, 1786.

On Saturday evening the 22d ult. eight of the prisoners, confined at the Castle, broke from their confinement, and made their escape to the main. The day following five of them were taken in a barn at Dorchester, and immediately re-conducted to the Castle. The ensuing night the three others were apprehended at Sharon, near Stoughton, and were also sent back to their place of confinement.

Richard Squire and John Matthews, the pirates, and Stephen Burroughs, a noted clerical character, were among the prisoners who made their escape from the Castle, as mentioned above. And on Saturday last, we are informed, the eight culprits shared among them the benefit of a distribution of 700 lashes.

On Monday evening last, a person, in passing from the Long-Wharf to

Dock-Square, was assaulted and knocked down, by a single villain, who robbed him of a box, containing a coat, two waistcoats, a pair of corduroy breeches, a piece of calico, in which was wrapped up three watches, and a letter containing money.

On Thursday last, at noon, seven fellows received the discipline of the post, in this town.

Curious list of punishments in the early days of New England. From "Salem Gazette," May 4, 1784.

The following (taken from a Boston paper of last week) is a collection of a few of the many curious punishments, inflicted for a variety of offences, among the old records of this Commonwealth.

Between 1630 and 1650.

Sir Richard Saltonstale fined four bushels of malt for his absence from court.

William Almy fined for taking away Mr. Glover's canoe without leave.

Josias Plastoree shall (for stealing four baskets of corn from the Indians) return them eight baskets again, be fined 5l. and hereafter to be called by the name of Josias, and not Mr. as formerly he used to be.

Joyce Bradwick shall give unto Alexander Beeks, 20s. for promising him marriage without her friends' consent, and now refusing to perform the same.

William James, for incontinency, was sentenced to be set in the bilboes at Boston and Salem, and bound in 20l.

Thomas Petet, for suspicion of slander, idleness and stubbornness, is to be severely whipt and kept in hold.

John Smith, of Medford, for swearing, being penitent, was set in bilboes.

Richard Turner, for being notoriously drunk, was fined 2l.

John Hoggs, for swearing God's foot, cursing his servant, wishing "a pox of God take you," was fined 5l.

Richard Ibrook, for tempting two or more maids to uncleanness, was fined 5l. to the country, and 20s. a piece to the two maids.

Thomas Makepeace, because of his novel disposition, was informed we were weary of him, unless he reformed.

Edward Palmer, for his extortion, taking 33s. 7d. for the plank and woodwork of Boston stocks, is fined 5l. and censured to be set an hour in the stocks.

John White is bound in 10l. to be of good behaviour, and not to come into the company of Bull's wife alone.

Thomas Lechford acknowledging he had overset himself and is sorry for it, promising to attend his calling, and not to meddle with controversies, was dismissed.

Sarah Hales was censured for her miscarriage to be carried to the gallows with a rope about her neck, and to sit upon the ladder, the rope end flung over the gallows, and after to be banished.

Wholesale sentences of death in London, in 1820.

At the October session of the Old Bailey, London, sentence of death was passed on thirty-seven persons, four of whom were females. Four were condemned for passing counterfeit notes, eleven for highway robberies, two for burglary, 11 for stealing in dwelling houses, 1 for horse-stealing, 2 for sacrilege, andc.

From the "Salem Mercury," July 28, 1788.

The following   Extraordinary Occurrence   is extracted from the European Magazine   for 1787.

SAMUEL BURT, convicted of forgery a few sessions since, was put to the bar, and informed that his Majesty, in his royal clemency, had been graciously pleased to extend his mercy to him on condition that he should be transported during his natural life. The prisoner bowed respectfully to the Court, and immediately addressed the Recorder with his "most humble and unfeigned thanks, for the kindness and humanity of the Recorder, the Sheriffs, and other gentlemen who had interested themselves in his favour, and who had so effectually represented his unhappy case to the throne, that his Majesty, whose humanity could only be equalled by his love of virtue, had extended his mercy; but however flattering the prospect of preserving life might be to a man in a different situation; yet that he, now he was sunk and degraded in society, was totally insensible of the blessing. Life was no longer an object with him, as it was utterly impossible that he could be joined in union with the person who was dearer to him than life itself. Under such circumstances, although he was truly sensible of his Majesty's goodness and clemency, yet he must positively decline the terms offered him; preferring death to the prolongation of a life which could not be otherwise than truly miserable." The whole Court was astonished at his address; and after consultation, Mr. Recorder remanded the prisoner back to the jail, to be brought up again the first day of next session.

The pillory appears to have been in use in Boston as lately as 1803; for we find in the "Chronicle" of that city that in March of that year Robert Pierpont, owner, and H.R. Story, master, of the brigantine "Hannah," for the crime of sinking the vessel at sea, and thus defrauding the underwriters (among whom were Joseph Taylor, Peter C. Brooks, Thomas Amory, David Greene, and Benjamin Bussey), were convicted before the Supreme Judicial Court, and the following sentence imposed: "That they should stand one hour in the Pillory in State Street on two several days, be confined in Prison for the term of two years, and pay Costs of Prosecution." Considering the magnitude of the crime, this was a light sentence. An underwriter in the "Chronicle" says: "It is a transaction exceeding in infamy all that has hitherto appeared in the commerce of our country."

Wholesale execution of pirates in Newport, R.I., in July, 1723.

CAPTURE OF PIRATES.

This year (1723) two Pirate sloops, called the Ranger and the Fortune, committed many piracies on the American Coast, having captured and sunk several vessels.—On the 6th of June, they captured a Virginia sloop, which they plundered and let go, who soon after fell in with his Majesty's Ship Grey Hound, Capt. Solgard, of 20 guns, who on being informed of the piracy, immediately went in pursuit of the Pirates, and on the 10th came up with them about 14 leagues south from the east end of Long Island. They mistaking her for a Merchant ship, immediately gave chase and commenced firing under the black flag.—The Grey Hound succeeded in capturing the Ranger, one of the sloops, after having 7 men wounded, but the other Pirate escaped. The Grey Hound and her prize arrived in the harbor of Newport, and the Pirates, 36 in number, were committed for trial.

Trial of the Pirates.

A Court of Admiralty, for the trial of Pirates, was held at Newport on the 10th, 11th and 12th of July. The Hon. William Dummer, Lt. Governor and Commander in Chief of the Province of Massachusetts Bay, President of the Court.

The thirty-six Pirates taken by Capt. Solgard, were tried, when Charles Harris, who acted as captain, and 25 of his men, were found guilty, and sentenced to suffer death, and 10 men were acquitted on the ground of having been forced into their service.

Execution of the Pirates.

On Friday the 19th of July, the 26 Pirates were taken to a place in Newport, called Bull's Point, (now Gravelly Point,) within the flux and reflux of the sea, and there hanged. The following are their names:—Charles Harris, Thomas Linnicar, Daniel Hyde, Stephen Mundon, Abraham Lacy, Edward Lawson, John Tomkins, Francis Laughton, John Fisgerald, Wm. Studfield, Owen Rice, Wm. Read, Wm. Blades, Tho's Hagget, Peter Cues, Wm. Jones, Edward Eaton, John Brown, James Sprinkly, Joseph Sound, Charles Church, John Waters, Tho's Powell, Joseph Libbey, Thomas Hazel, John Bright.

The Pirates were all young men, most of them were natives of England, Wm. Blades was from Rhode Island and Thomas Powell from Wethersfield, (Conn.); after the execution, their bodies were taken to the north end of Goat Island, and buried on the shore, between high and low water mark.

As this was the most extensive execution of Pirates that ever took place at one time in the Colonies, it was attended by a vast multitude from every part of New England.

From the Salem Observer, Nov. 11, 1843.

Description of "Villains" in the "Boston Post-Boy," Dec. 12, 1763.

Tuesday last a Gang of Villains were apprehended at a House in Roxbury, and brought to Town and committed to Goal, they have been concerned in the late Robberies here, and 'tis suspected in some of those towards Pennsylvania, for which Reason it will be proper to advertise their Names, with some Description of them, which are as follows, viz.

William Robinson, a tall slim fellow, about 5 Feet 7 inches high, wears a blue Surtout Coat with metal Buttons, and his Hat commonly flopt before, and an old laced Waistcoat, has short curled black Hair; when he speaks he seems jaw-fallen and very effeminate, is about 35 Years of Age, walks much like a Foot-pad, and has a comely Woman with him whom he calls his Wife.—John Cassady, a middling siz'd Fellow much pock-broken, square-shoulder'd, wears a Wig upon the yellow cast, and has a very guilty Countenance, is about 40 Years of Age, and calls himself a Shoe-maker.— John Willson, a short young Fellow, about 21 Years of Age, wears a blue Surtout Coat, and short black Hair, of a pale Countenance, and calls himself a Sail-maker.—George Sears, a well-set Fellow, with a comely Face, black Hair twisted with a black Ribbon, and says he serv'd 3 Years to an Attorney in England.

In the "Essex Gazette," Nov. 12, 1771, is the following news from England:—

A Correspondent expresses great Surprise and indignation at the Disproportion of Punishments in this Country. He says he read in a News paper that two Men were hanged together last Month in Kent, one of whom had committed a barbarous Murder on his Wife, and the other had stolen three Shillings and Sixpence. In the same Paper there followed immediately another Paragraph, that a Woman had been only whipped for stealing little Children and burning their Eyes out.

At this day we believe it is the custom of the English authorities to treat all prisoners alike, whatever the charges against them may be. It seems as if they were desirous of degrading men as much as possible. Mr. John Boyle O'Reilly, a poet and gentleman of culture, who was unfortunately a political prisoner, was chained to a wife-murderer. And this the English call "justice,"—as if there could be no difference in offences!

Severe punishment used to be inflicted for the crime of passing counterfeit coin. The "Essex Gazette," April 23, 1771, under news from Newport, April 15, says,—

William Carlisle was convicted of passing counterfeit Dollars, and sentenced to stand One Hour in the Pillory, on Little-Rest Hill, next Friday, to have both Ears cropped, to be branded on both Cheeks with the Letter R, to pay a Fine of One hundred Dollars and Cost of Prosecution, and to stand committed till Sentence performed.

The letter R probably meant "rogue." The same account states that—

"Last Wednesday Evening one Mr. ——, of this Town (Newport), was catched by a Number of Persons in Disguise, placed on an old Horse, and paraded through the principal Streets for about an Hour as a Warning to all bad Husbands."

In the "Massachusetts Gazette," Sept. 8, 1786, we find an account of the Dutch mode of executions.

NEW-JERSEY.

Elizabeth-Town, Aug. 16. The little influence which our present mode of executing criminals has in deterring others from the commission of the same crimes, arises from a want of solemnity and terrifick circumstances on such occasions. It is not the mere loss of life which has so much a tendency to affect the spectator, as the dreadful apparatus, the awful preliminaries, which ought to attend publick executions; whose justifiable purposes is the prevention of crimes, and not the inflicting torment on the criminal. A variety of particulars might be adopted respecting the dress of the condemned, the solemnity of the procession to the place of execution, and the apparatus there, to throw horrour on the scene without in reality giving the unhappy victim a more painful exit. The Dutch have a mode of execution which is well calculated to inspire terror, without putting the sufferer to extraordinary pain. The criminal is placed on a scaffold, opposite to the gigantick figure of a woman, with arms extended, filled with spikes, or long sharpened nails, and a dagger pointed from her breast, she is gradually moved towards him by machinery for the purpose, till he gets within her embrace, when her arms encircle him, and the dagger is pressed through his heart. This is vulgarly called among them, kissing the Yssrow, or woman, and excites more terror in the breasts of the populace than any other mode of punishment.

Inhabitants of Boston severely punished (on paper) in April, 1774, for destruction of the tea.

A Curious Historical Item. In a recent English Chronological work, under the article of "Tea," we found the following brief notice of the American Revolution: "Tea destroyed at Boston by the inhabitants, 1773, in abhorrence of English Taxes; for which they were severely punished by the English Parliament, in April, 1774."

Salem Observer, April 28, 1827.

Sentences of death for robbery, May 6, 1788.

The Mulatto who, some time since, robbed Mr. Bacon, on the Cambridge road, was, at the late term of the Supreme Court at Concord, convicted of the crime, and had sentence of death pronounced against him.

Thursday next is the day appointed for the execution of the two Taylors, for the robbery of Mr. Cunningham, on Boston-Neck.

Captain Phillips, of the British army, whipped in New York in 1784.

PHILADELPHIA, February 4, 1784.

On Saturday last, was whipped at the cart's tail, for robbery, one of George the Third's pretty subjects. This fellow, who now goes by the name of Captain Phillips, under his good friend Sir Harry Clinton, learned such a knack of thieving while he commanded a whale-boat along this coast, under his good master, that now, having lost his protection, he and a number more of those lads called Loyalists are swarming amongst us, and have set up business in a small way; and though many of them may not choose to steal themselves, yet, by harbouring and encouraging others, may do much mischief to the good inhabitants of these states.

Salem Gazette.

Sentences at the Supreme Court.

BOSTON, March 22, 1784.

At the Supreme Judicial Court, lately held here, the following persons were arraigned, viz.

Thomas Hastings, indicted for selling corrupt swine's flesh, was found guilty.—He was sentenced to pay a fine of twelve pounds for the use of the Commonwealth, recognize himself as principal in the sum of thirty pounds, with sufficient surety or sureties in the like sum, for his keeping the peace and being of good behaviour for the term of one year, pay costs of prosecution, and stand committed till sentence be performed.

John Boyd, for stealing, pled guilty:—sentenced to pay to the person injured, treble the value of the goods stolen, receive 20 stripes at the public whipping post, sit on the gallows one hour with a rope about his neck, pay costs of prosecution, and stand committed till sentence be performed.—He was, upon another indictment for theft, sentenced to pay treble damages, whipped 15 stripes, and pay costs of prosecution.—Upon declaring himself unable to pay damages, he was for the first offence sentenced to be sold for 9 months, and for the second, 2 months.

Lewis Humphries, for stealing, pled guilty:—sentenced to pay treble damages, receive 20 stripes, sit on the gallows one hour with a rope about his neck, pay costs of prosecution, and stand committed till sentence be performed.—Upon declaring himself unable to pay damages, was sentenced to be sold for the term of 5 years.

William Padley, for an assault upon his wife, with an intent to kill her, was tried, found guilty, and sentenced to sit on the gallows one hour, there to receive 30 stripes, pay costs of prosecution, and stand committed till sentence be performed.

Sentences by the Supreme Judicial Court at Salem, Nov. 18, 1786.

At the Supreme Judicial Court, holden in this town, for the county of Essex, which adjourned on Thursday last, several persons, criminally indicted, were convicted and severally sentenced. Isaac Coombs, an Indian, was found guilty, at last June term, at Ipswich, of murdering his wife; at which time a motion was made to the Court, in arrest of judgment, on which the Court suspended giving judgment thereon until this term; but the said motion being overruled, the Court gave judgment of death against him. Besides the sentence of the Indian, as above, Thomas Kendry, for breaking into the store of Israel Bartlet, and stealing sundry goods, was sentenced, on his confession, to pay said Bartlet £33-9-6, to sit on the gallows one hour with a rope about his neck, to be whipped 30 stripes, and confined to hard labour on Castle-island two years.

Thomas Atwood and John Ransum, for breaking open the store of Knott Pedrick, and stealing dry fish, were each sentenced to pay said Pedrick £40-5-0, to sit one hour on the gallows, be whipped 36 stripes, and confined to labour on Castle-island 3 years.

John Smith, for stealing goods from Abner Perkins, was sentenced to pay said Perkins £18-4-0, and be whipped 25 stripes.

The same John Smith, for breaking open a sloop, and stealing goods of John Brooks, was sentenced to pay said Brooks £16-8-0, to sit one hour on the gallows, be whipped 30 stripes, and confined 18 months on Castle-island.

John Scudder, for stealing from Eli Gale, was sentenced to pay said Gale £5-2-0, or if unable to pay, to be disposed of by him, in service, to any person, for 2 months.

Joseph Ballard, for stealing a horse from Thomas Dodge, was sentenced to pay £30, be whipped 20 stripes, pay costs, andc. and, if unable to pay, that said Dodge may dispose of him in service to any person for two years.

Calvin Newhall was indicted for assaulting Deborah Sarker, a negro woman, with intent to commit a rape upon her. He pleaded not guilty; and the jury found him guilty of the assault, but whether with an intent to ravish they could not agree; whereupon the Attorney General would no further prosecute for said intent to ravish; and the Court ordered that said Calvin should be whipped 10 stripes, and recognize in £60, with sufficient surety in a like sum, to be of good behaviour for 3 months, and pay costs.

Punishment in 1644 for criticising the preacher and the music, and for sleeping in "meeting."

The Hon. Wm. D. Northend, in a very interesting and valuable address before the Essex Bar Association, Dec. 8, 1885, mentions the following among other cases taken from the Essex County Court Records:—

"In 1644 William Hewes and John his son, for terming such as sing in the congregation fools, and William Hewes also for charging Reverend Mr. Corbitt with falsehood in his doctrine, were ordered to pay a fine of fifty shillings each, and to make humble confession in a public meeting at Lynn."

William Hewes and his son were probably only criticising the music and the preaching in the "meeting-house." If people nowadays were fined for similar offences, the county would grow so rich that there would be no necessity for the present heavy tax.

"In 1643 Roger Scott, for repeated sleeping in meeting on the Lord's Day, and for striking the person who waked him, was, at Salem, sentenced to be severely whipped."

It must be borne in mind that people in those days were not allowed to stay at home on the Lord's Day and do their sleeping there. Staying at home on Sunday is a modern innovation.

From the Massachusetts Colony Records, quoted by Mr. Northend, we learn that in March, 1761, Sir Christopher Gardner, who had passed much of his time "with roystering Morton of Merry Mount," and who was living with a lady he called his cousin, upon receipt by the Governor of information of two wives in England "whom he has carelessly left behind," after a long pursuit was captured and sent back to England.

It would seem, then, that there must have been, judging from this example, in "high places" some "indiscretions" and "unpleasant" gossip early in our history.

Mr. Northend finds that at "the same date one Nich. Knopp, for pretending to cure scurvy by water of no value, which he sold at a very dear rate, was ordered to pay a fine of five pounds or be whipped, and made liable to an action by any person to whom he had sold the water."

How would such a decree work in our day, if applied to the makers or venders of all the "water of no value" which is advertised on the fences and barns alongside of our railroads and highways?

Mr. Northend, speaking of the severity of the early laws, says:—

"The criminal laws were taken principally from the Mosaic code; and although many of them at the present day seem harsh and cruel, yet as a whole they were very much milder than the criminal laws of England at the time, and the number of capital offences was greatly reduced."

CURIOUS PUNISHMENTS IN SCHOOLS.

In some of the old schools in Salem (no doubt it was the same in other places) the teachers whose business it was to teach youths the "three R's,"—Reading, 'Riting, and 'Rithmetic,—were too apt to be occupied, as we have been told, in scolding, devising or practising some mode of punishment. We remember hearing of a school where the master kept a long cane pole (something like a fishing-rod) which he used for the purpose of reaching boys who needed correction; on account of the length of the pole he was enabled to do business without leaving his seat. It was never suspected at the time how lazy this master was.

Another teacher kept for use as a punishment a common walnut, which when occasion required he first put into the mouth of a colored boy, and after it had remained there for five minutes or so, it was taken out and put into the mouth of the white boy, who was thus to be punished by holding it in his mouth for a certain length of time. This same teacher had a round smooth stone, weighing perhaps ten or fifteen pounds, which very small boys were required to hold in their arms for some time, and stand up straight before the whole school. These with a good rattan and a cowhide furnished this master's equipment for teaching.

There was another master who had what he called "the mansion of misery," which was simply a line drawn with chalk on the floor in front of his desk, where for trifling offences such as whispering, etc., scholars were required to "toe the mark," standing perfectly still and upright for a long time. This was often to a little boy painful enough. This master had a stock of cowhides and rattans besides.

Another teacher, a woman, had the floor of the school-room kept very clean; consequently no boys were allowed to come in at all with heavy boots, and the other children in wet weather were compelled to remove their boots and shoes and put on slippers before entrance. If any of the scholars were too small to take off and put on their own boots they were punished by being "blindfolded" and stood upon a cricket in the middle of the floor. Apparently the worst offence scholars could be guilty of was to bring in mud or wet upon the polished floor of the school-room. At this school one very small boy who wore high boots, but who was unable to take them off without assistance, having been punished for his "stubbornness," was taken away from the school by his parents, who resented such an act of injustice and oppression. The "school-marm," however, said she would rather lose all her scholars than have any mud or wet upon her floor.

These cases are simply curious. It may be doubted whether we can in this country show anything so bad as the record furnished by Dickens in describing some of the schools of England.

THE BRANK.

An instrument of punishment formerly much used in England, but never, we think, introduced into this country, called the "brank," or "scold's bridle," or "gossip's bridle," is thus described by Mr. L. Jewitt, F.S.A., in Mr. William Andrews's "Book of Oddities,"—a very interesting and instructive book recently published in London:—

"It consisted of a kind of crown or framework of iron, which was locked upon the head, and was armed in front with a gag, a plate, or a sharp cutting knife or point, which was placed in the poor woman's mouth so as to prevent her moving her tongue, or it was so placed that if she moved it or attempted to speak, the tongue was cut in a most frightful manner. With this cage upon her head, and with the gag firmly pressed and locked against her tongue, the miserable creature, whose sole offence, perhaps, was that she had raised her voice in defence of her social rights against a brutal and besotted husband, or had spoken honest truth of some one high in office in the town, was paraded through the streets, led by a chain held in the hand of the bellman, the beadle, or the constable, or, chained to the pillory, the whipping-post, or market-cross, was subjected to every conceivable insult and degradation, without even the power left her of asking for mercy or of promising amendment for the future; and when the punishment was over, she was turned out from the town hall (or other place where the brutal punishment had been inflicted), maimed, disfigured, faint, and degraded, to be the subject of comment and jeering amongst her neighbors, and to be reviled by her persecutors."

Mr. Andrews adds that the use of the brank was not sanctioned by law, but was altogether illegal; and he concludes his remarks on the subject by saying that "to everybody it must be a matter of deep regret that the instrument should ever have been used at all."

Dr. Henry Heginbotham, of Stockport, England, says in speaking of the brank preserved in that town: "There is no evidence of its having been actually used for many years; but there is testimony to the fact that within the last forty years the brank was brought to a termagant market-woman, who was effectually silenced by its threatened application."

It is hard for those of us who live in New England to-day to believe that such cruelties were ever practised in a Christian land; but the evidence is too conclusive to admit of doubt. Mr. Andrews, in the book referred to, gives engravings of a dozen or more different kinds of branks and bridles which can now be seen in England and Scotland. At Congleton, Cheshire, a woman for scolding and abusing the town officers had the "town bridle" put upon her, and was led through every street in the town, as lately as the year 1824.

It is said that Chaucer wrote these lines:

"But for my daughter Julian,
I would she were well bolted with a Bridle,
That leaves her work to play the clack,
And lets her wheel stand idle;
For it serves not for she-ministers,
Farriers nor Furriers,
Cobblers nor Button-makers,
To descant on the Bible."

Mr. Andrews has confined his account of curious punishments mainly to England and Scotland. Our Puritan ancestors must, we think, have seen some of the instruments of torture here described, and perhaps some of our great-great, etc., grandmothers may have been "ducked" or "silenced by a brank" many years before the sailing of the "Mayflower" or the "Lyon" or the "Angel Gabriel."

It was once the custom in New England for a sermon to be preached before the prisoner upon the day of his execution. In the "Massachusetts Gazette," Dec. 26, 1786, is the following notice:—

Salem, Dec. 23. Thursday last, being the day appointed for the execution of Isaac Coombs, an Indian, with whose crime and sentence the publick have before been made acquainted, the unfortunate criminal was in the forenoon conducted to the Tabernacle, where a Sermon, which we are told was well adapted to the melancholy occasion, was preached by the Rev. Mr. Spalding, from Luke xviii. 13,—"God be merciful to me a sinner!" After which he was returned to the prison. Between the hours of 2 and 3 in the afternoon, he was guarded to the place of execution by a company of 40 volunteers (consisting principally of the members of the Artillery Company lately formed in this town, and commanded by Captain Zadock Buffinton) under the direction of the proper civil officers. The Rev. Mr. Hopkins prayed at the gallows; and at 3 o'clock the cart was led off, and the unhappy sufferer made the expiation which the law required for his horrid and unnatural crime.

His behaviour, through the whole, was firm, but decent, penitent and devotional.

This is the only execution which has taken place in the county of Essex for near 15 years, and but the second since about the close of the last century. The concourse of people was consequently great; and the general decorum which was observed, evinced their sympathy for a suffering individual of the species.

The conduct of the military corps was highly applauded.

On the way to execution the following paper was delivered to the Rev. Mr. Bentley, by one of the officers, with a request from Isaac, that he would read it publickly at the place of execution, at the time he should signify to him; accordingly, when the sheriff told the criminal his time was expired, as the last thing, he made the motion, and it was read to the people. As it is so contradictory to the declaration he made before of himself, we have printed it verbatim as it is written, to avoid the charge of any alteration.

"I Who has ben Called by the name of Isaac Cumbs Being Now Called to the place of Execution in the 39th year of my age, I Declare I was born at South hampton Long Island and am a Native of the said South hampton and my Right Name is John Peters and Leaving the said South hampton about 14 years ago, and comeing to St. Mertains Vineyard am Ben a traveller Eversince till I have Now arrived to this unhappy Place of Execution My advice is to all Spectators to Refrain from lying Stealing and all suchlike things But in particular Not to Break the Sabbath of the Lord or Game at Cerds or get Drunk as I have Don. this is My advice and more in particular to mixt coulard people and youths of Every Kind. May the Blessing of god Desend upon you all Amen."

In the "Essex Gazette," Jan. 15, 1771, is an advertisement of a poem upon an execution.

To be sold at the Printing-Office, Salem.

A POEM on the Execution of

William Shaw, at Springfield, December 13, 1770, for the Murder of

Edward East, in Springfield Gaol.

We have seen an account of an execution where a sermon was preached at the prisoner's request.

BOSTON COMMON AS A PLACE OF EXECUTION.

Boston Common was formerly often used for such a purpose. Quakers were hanged there in the middle of the seventeenth century, and we find in the "Salem Mercury" for Tuesday, Nov. 27, 1787, that the previous Thursday one John Sheehan was executed for burglary in this noted locality. Sheehan was a native of Cork in Ireland. With its cows and its executions, the Common must have presented a somewhat different appearance in those days from what it does at this time.

British convicts shipped to America in 1788.

Last week arrived at Fisher's Island, the brig Nancy, belonging to this port, Capt. Robert W—— (a half-pay British officer) master, and landed his cargo, consisting of 140 convicts, taken out of the British jails. Capt. W. it is said, received 5l. sterling a head from government for this job; and, we hear, he is distributing them about the country. Stand to it, houses, stores, andc., these gentry are acquainted with the business. Quere, whether a suit of T—— — and F—— should not be provided for Capt. W. as a suitable compliment for this piece of service done his country?

Salem Mercury, July 15, 1788.

From the "Salem Gazette," 1784.

July 30. During the long reign of Queen Elizabeth, it does not appear on record, that forty persons suffered death for crimes against the community, treason only excepted.

BOSTON, September 16, 1784.

At the Supreme Court held here on Thursday last, Direck Grout was tried for Burglary, and found guilty: sentence has not yet been passed upon him.

The following prisoners were also tried last week for various thefts, found guilty, and received sentence, viz.

Cornelius Arie, to be whipt 25 stripes, and set one hour on the gallows.

Thomas Joice, to be whipt 25 stripes, and branded.

William Scott, to be whipt 25 stripes, and set one hour on the gallows.

John Goodbread, and Edward Cooper, 15 stripes each.

James Campbell, to be whipt 30 stripes, and set one hour on the gallows.

Michael Tool, to be whipt 20 stripes.

Three notorious villains yet remain to be tried for burglary, and several others for theft.

BOSTON, September 27.

Thursday last ten notorious villains received publick whipping, after which three of them were escorted, with halters round their necks, to the gallows, on which they sat one hour. They are again committed for costs, andc.

"Massachusetts Gazette," 1786.

Johnson Green was executed, on Thursday last, at Worcester, for burglary. A greater thief and burglar was perhaps never hanged in this country.

From "Massachusetts Centinel," Oct. 6, 1786.

BACKS "DRESS'D."

HARTFORD, October 2.

On Wednesday last, David Stillman, John Hawley and Thomas Gibbs were committed to jail in this city, for counterfeiting and passing publick securities; and on Thursday last, Jonathan Densmore, of East-Hartford, was committed for stealing a horse. Stillman and Hawley belong to the county of Hampshire, state of Massachusetts. They are now in a fair way to have their grievances (and backs) dress'd and re-dress'd.

From "Massachusetts Gazette," May 15, 1786.

NEW-YORK, May 6.

Extract of a letter from Washington (North-Carolina), March 27.

"On Thursday last made his appearance in this town, a certain John Hamlen, who, in the late war, left the state of Maryland, and joined the enemies of America. After joining them, he fitted out a galley, and cruised in the Delaware and Chesapeak, where he was very successful in capturing a number of American vessels. He was very fond of exercising every species of cruelty on those unhappy people who fell into his hands; among other things, he took great delight in cutting off the ears of some, and noses of others. Unluckily for him he was known by some honest Jack Tars, belonging to vessels in this harbour, who, in the time of the war, had been made prisoners by him; these honest fellows very kindly furnished him with a coat of Tar and Feathers; and that he might not in a short time forget them, they took off one of his ears; they then kindly shewed him the way out of town, without doing him any further injury.—It is supposed he will bend his course for Newbern, and endeavour to take a passage in some vessel bound to the northern states."

FROM THE AUGUSTA CHRONICLE.

A GEORGIA SHREW.

"Why, sirs, I trust I may have leave to speak,
And speak I will; I am no child, no babe:
Your betters have endur'd me say my mind;
And if you cannot, best you stop your ears."

The Grand Jury of Burke have presented Mary Cammell as a common scold and disturber of the peaceable inhabitants of that county.[1] We do not know the penalty, or if there be any attached to the offence of scolding: but for the information of our Burke neighbours, we would inform them that the late lamented and distinguished Judge Early decided, some years since, when a modern Xantippe was brought before him, that she should undergo the punishment of lustration, by immersion three several times in the Oconee. Accordingly she was confined to the tail of a cart, and, accompanied by the hooting of the mob, conducted to the river, where she was publickly ducked, in conformity with the sentence of the court. Should this punishment be awarded Mary Cammell, we hope, however, it may be attended with a more salutary effect than in the case we have just alluded to—the unruly subject of which, each time as she arose from the watery element, impiously exclaimed, with a ludicrous gravity of countenance, "glory to G—d."

Boston Palladium, 1819.

[1]

She must have been an extraordinary scold to have disturbed a large county, where the houses are perhaps a half mile apart.

Criminals after a whipping sent to the Castle to make nails. From "Salem Mercury," Nov. 25, 1786.

Four convicts, doomed by the Superiour Court, at their late session here, to the useful branch of nail making at the Castle, yesterday morning took their departure hence, to enter on their new employment, having, with others, previously received the discipline of the post.

A REVEREND FORGER.

The "Providence Gazette" is our authority for the following obituary notice:—

Died in March, 1805, in Wayne County, N.C., Rev. Thomas Hines, an itinerant preacher. A Newbern paper says: "In the saddle-bags of this servant of God and Mammon were found his Bible and a complete apparatus for the stamping and milling of Dollars."

THE SUPREME JUDICIAL COURT

Was held at Ipswich on Tuesday last. At this Court the noted Josiah Abbot was found guilty of knowingly passing a forged and altered State Note, and was sentenced to pay a fine of 40l. in 20 days; if not then paid, to be set in the pillory.—[The penalty of such an offence against the United States is DEATH.]

The same person was found guilty of a fraud, in stealing a summons, after it had been left by an officer, by reason of which he recovered a judgment by default, and was sentenced to pay a fine of 15l. in 20 days; if not then paid, to be whipped.

Salem Gazette, June 25, 1793.

In a paper of 1819 is mentioned the singular case of a man literally condemned "to eat his own words."

INCREDIBLE PUNISHMENT.

"A great book is a great evil," said an ancient writer,—an axiom which an unfortunate Russian author felt to his cost. "Whilst I was at Moscow," says a pleasant traveller, "a quarto volume was published in favor of the liberties of the people,—a singular subject when we consider the place where the book was printed. In this work the iniquitous venality of the public functionaries, and even the conduct of the sovereign, was scrutinized and censured with great freedom. Such a book, and in such a country, naturally attracted general notice, and the offender was taken into custody. After being tried in a very summary way, his production was determined to be a libel, and the writer was condemned to eat his own words. The singularity of such a sentence induced me to see it put into execution. A scaffold was erected in one of the most public streets of the city; the imperial provost, the magistrates, the physicians and surgeons of the Czar attended; the book was separated from its binding, the margin cut off, and every leaf rolled up like a lottery ticket when taken out of the wheel at Guildhall. The author was then served with them leaf by leaf by the provost, who put them into his mouth, to the no small diversion of the spectators; he was obliged to swallow this unpalatable food on pain of the knout,—in Russia more dreadful than death. As soon as the medical gentlemen were of opinion that he had received into his stomach as much at the time as was consistent with his safety, the transgressor was sent back to prison, and the business resumed the two following days. After three very hearty but unpleasant meals, I am convinced by ocular proof that every leaf of the book was actually swallowed."

Lon. Pa.

Boston Palladium.

Here is a clever mode of punishing a wife-beater without the aid of counsel:—

A woman in New-York, who had been beaten by her husband, finding him fast asleep, sewed him up in the bed-clothes, and in that situation thrashed him soundly.

Salem Observer, April 24, 1827.

Conviction of a common scold, Sept. 11, 1821; sentence not reported.

Common Scold.—Catharine Fields was indicted and convicted for being a common scold. The trial was excessively amusing, from the variety of testimony and the diversified manner in which this Xantippe pursued her virulent propensities. "Ruder than March wind, she blew a hurricane;" and it was given in evidence that after having scolded the family individually, the bipeds and quadrupeds, the neighbours, hogs, poultry, and geese, she would throw the window open at night to scold the watchmen. Her countenance was an index to her temper,—sharp, peaked, sallow, and small eyes. To be sentenced on Saturday week.—Nat. Adv.

Women Gossips.—Among the many ordinances promulgated at St. Helena in 1709, we find the following:—

Whereas several idle, gossiping women make it their business to go from house [to house] about the island, inventing and spreading false and scandalous reports of the good people thereof, and thereby sow discord and debate among neighbors, and often between men and their wives, to the great grief and trouble of all good and quiet people, and to the utter extinguishing of all friendship, amity, and good neighborhood: for the punishment and suppression whereof, and to the intent that all strife may be ended, charity revived, and friendship continued,—we do order that, if any woman, from henceforward, shall be convicted of tale bearing, mischief making, scolding, drunkenness, or any other notorious vice, that they shall be punished by ducking, or whipping, or such other punishment as their crimes or transgressions shall deserve, or as the Governor and Council shall think fit.

Essex Register, 1820.

IMPRISONMENT FOR DEBT.

The following scrap from a Boston paper of 1819 has reference to an old method which creditors frequently resorted to in dealing with troublesome, and no doubt oftentimes unfortunate, debtors.

CHRISTMAS DAY.

On this most glorious "Day of Days" there are in gaol for debt, in this town, the following persons, viz.:

1 Head of a Family for —	—	9 94
1 — do. —	—	8 12½
1 — do. —	—	14 00
1 — do. —	—	9 61
1 — do. —	—	11 68
1 — do. —	—	27 00
1 — do. —	—	7 75
1 — do. for schooling his children,	11 25	
1 — do. discharged	1 88!!!	

Who among the opulent is willing to restore a Father to his Family and Christmas Fire Side?

Sometimes debtors were not actually imprisoned, but were confined to what was called the "limits of the jail;" that is, certain streets within a specified distance of the jail. The writer distinctly remembers, when a boy, of having a man pointed out to him, of whom it was said he had refused to pay his debts, and so was only allowed to go at large "within the limits of the jail."

The law under which persons were imprisoned for debt was abolished in Massachusetts many years ago.

Somewhere about the year 1822 the tread-mill was introduced into England. It was recommended by the "Society for the Improvement of Prison Discipline." It was the invention of Mr. Cubitt, of Ipswich, in England, and probably at that time or soon after it was used in this country. Some years since there was one, as we are informed, at the Massachusetts State prison at Charlestown.

The Tread-Mill.—We publish to-day an interesting description of the Tread-Mill, (a new invented Machine to enforce industry in Prisons,) accompanied by a Plate representing the same, for the use of which we are indebted to the politeness of the editor of the Gazette. The introduction of these Mills into the English prisons is said to have produced much good, and the experiment is about to be tried in this country. The corporation of the city of New-York are building one in the yard of their Penitentiary. One of the late London papers announces the singular fact that on the 12th of September, at the Town-hall, Southwark, there was no charge, either of felony, misdemeanor, or assault, within the extensive district, of five parishes, from the night before. Crimes of all descriptions had lessened very much; and this decrease, it is said, is owing entirely to the heavy and tedious labor upon the prisoners at the mill. Orders had been given for the erection of several more in England.

Salem Register, 1822.

Description of the Tread Mill

Recommended by the Society for the Improvement of Prison Discipline.

The annexed engraving exhibits a party of prisoners in the act of working one of the tread wheels of the Discipline Mill invented by Mr. Cubitt, of Ipswich, and recently erected at the House of Correction for the county of Surrey, situated at Brixton. The view is taken from a corner of one of the ten airing yards of the prison, all of which radiate from the Governor's house in the centre, so that from the window of his room he commands a complete view into all the yards. A building behind the tread wheel shed is the mill house, containing the necessary machinery for grinding corn and dressing the flour, also rooms for storing it, andc. On the right side of this building a pipe passes up to the roof, on which is a large cast iron reservoir, capable of holding some thousand gallons of water, for the use of the prison. This reservoir is filled by means of forcing pump machinery below, connected with the principal axis which works the machinery of the mill; this axis or shaft passes under the pavement of the several yards, and working by means of universal joints, at every turn communicates with the tread wheel of each class.

The wheel, which is represented in the centre of the engraving, is exactly similar to a common water wheel; the treadboards upon its circumference are, however, of considerable length, so as to allow sufficient standing room for a row of from ten to twenty persons upon the wheel. Their weight, the first moving power of the machine, produces the greatest effect when applied upon the circumference of the wheel at or near the level of its axle; to secure therefore this mechanical advantage, a screen of boards is fixed up in an inclined position above the wood, in order to prevent the prisoners from climbing or stepping up higher than the level required. A hand rail is fixed upon this screen, by holding which they retain their upright position upon the revolving wheel, the nearest side of which is exposed to view in the plate, in order to represent its cylindrical form much more distinctly than could otherwise have been done. In the original, however, both sides are closely boarded up, so that the prisoners have no access to the interior of the wheel, and all risk of injury whatever is prevented.

Tread-mill

By means of steps the gang of prisoners ascend at one end, and when the requisite number range themselves upon the wheel, it commences its revolutions. The effort, then, to every individual is simply that of ascending an endless flight of steps, their combined weight acting upon every successive stepping board precisely as a stream of water upon the float boards of a water wheel.

During this operation each prisoner gradually advances from the end at which he mounted towards the opposite end of the wheel, from whence the last man taking his turn descends for rest, another prisoner immediately mounting as before to fill up the number required, without stopping the machine. The interval of rest may then be portioned to each man by regulating the number of those required to work the wheel with the whole number of the gang; thus if twenty-four are obliged to be upon the wheel, it will give to each man intervals of rest amounting to twelve minutes in every hour of labor. Again, by varying the number of men upon the wheel, or the work inside the mill, so as to increase or diminish its velocity, the degree of hard labor or exercise for the prisoners may also be regulated. At Brixton, the diameter of the wheel being five feet, and revolving twice in a minute, the space stepped over by each man is 2193 feet.

From the Salem Register.

Travelling on Sunday. At the session of the U. States Circuit Court at New-Haven (Conn.) last week came on the trial of Foster vs. Huntington. This was a prosecution instituted by Dr. Foster, of New-York, against Deacon Eliphalet Huntington, a Constable of Lebanon (Conn.), for arresting plaintiff's wife on Sunday, the 10th of July, 1831, at 3 o'clock in the afternoon, and detained her at an inn until sun-down, and then released her on condition of appearing the next morning to answer for violating the Sabbath. Mrs. Foster was travelling from New York City to her father's in Lebanon for her health, and had arrived at East Haddam on the morning of Sunday, and took the regular conveyance connected with the steamboat, and had arrived near the meeting-house in Lebanon at the time she was stopped, and was in sight of her father's (Dr. Sweet) house, when arrested.

The action was for false imprisonment, and it was contended by the plaintiffs,—1st, That Mrs. Foster was travelling from necessity and charity, and so within the exception of the statute. 2d, That the defendant could not justify himself as Constable unless he carried the person apprehended under the Sabbath law before a Justice. 3d, That as Constable he had no power to detain, and that he did not disclose his authority as Constable to arrest. And 4th, that the Sabbath law and its provisions are unconstitutional.

Judge Thompson charged the jury that the words "necessity and charity" in our statute mean not physical necessity, but moral fitness and propriety, and that it was incumbent on Mrs. Foster to show that there was some necessity of this kind operating on her when she left New York—she knowing that her regular route would require travelling on Sunday; but that a Constable when he arrests, must carry the prisoner, under the law, before a Justice, and then he has done his duty; and as the defendant had not done it in this case, he was liable. The Judge further expressed a decided opinion that the law was constitutional, and that before he could say a law was otherwise which had been acquiesced in so long, he should require the strongest reasons to be shown. As to what constituted an arrest, the Judge remarked that force was not required, or a touching, but it must be a detention professed to be done by authority and an exercise of authority; which, he observed, was clearly proved in the present case. The damages should give at least the actual injury and something as smart money, if there was any bad motive. This the Judge said did not appear, but the officer seemed to be impressed with a desire to discharge his duty.

The jury returned a verdict of 125 dollars damages and costs for the plaintiffs.—New-Haven Reg.

[This was a case tried under the statute of Connecticut against the right of unnecessary travelling on the Sabbath. The result appears to be very remarkable. In the first place, we consider the Law itself to be clearly unconstitutional, and we have never had the slightest doubt that if the question ever goes to Washington, the Supreme Court will declare it unconstitutional, and reverse the decision of the Connecticut Court.— Boston Centinel.]

Salem Observer, May 4, 1833.

The ridiculous practice here recorded does not appear to have gained a foothold in America. It would have been, to say the least, less harmful in its effects than the hanging of witches or the whipping of Quakers.

Prosecutions against Animals. The second number of the American Jurist, just published, contains a curious article relating to the prosecutions formerly instituted against animals, and for whom counsel was sometimes assigned by the Court, in the same manner as is now done in cases of capital felony. The first case mentioned is a prosecution of some rats in the Bishopric of Autun, in France. They had become so mischievous that a bill in due form was filed against the rats, and a summons issued for their appearance before the Court. The Judge, unwilling to take advantage of their default, appointed an advocate to plead for them, and he managed their cause so adroitly that by means of this prosecution he obtained an elevation to the highest honor of his profession. In another case counsel

was appointed to defend some caterpillars who had drawn upon themselves the vengeance of the law; but the ingenious arguments of their advocate availed nothing, and the caterpillars fell under the censure of a spiritual Court, who ordered adjuration, prayers, and sprinkling of holy water.
Salem Observer, May 9, 1829.
A very full and interesting account of this subject can be found in a recent number of the "Popular Science Monthly."
Arrest in Connecticut for teaching colored children.
Connecticut Barbarism. We have been permitted to read a letter from Miss Prudence Crandall, who is actually confined in jail in the town of Brooklyn, Conn., for teaching colored misses to read and write!
The letter from Miss Crandall is dated "Brooklyn Jail, close confinement, June 28, 1833." Miss Crandall simply relates that she was arrested on the 27th, with her sister, by Mr. Cady, the Sheriff of the County, and examined before Justice Rufus Adams. Miss Crandall was found guilty of teaching blacks to read, and was thereupon bound over, in the sum of $150, to appear at the Superior Court holden at Brooklyn on the second Tuesday of August next.
Miss Crandall was sent to the county jail and put into the cell which had been occupied by Watkins the murderer. At the close of her letter she says, "If all the prisoners are as happy as I am, I can assure you they do not bear much mental suffering."
The friends of Miss Crandall were preparing to give the bond necessary for her release.
Salem Observer, July 6, 1833.
Innholders prosecuted as lately as 1824 for the crime of entertaining on the Lord's Day.
John F. Trueman and Almoran Holmes, licensed Innholders, convicted on several indictments for entertaining two inhabitants of Boston on the Lord's Day, they not being travellers, strangers, or lodgers, were sentenced according to the act of 1796, each to pay a fine of $6 66 and costs of prosecution.
Boston Telegraph.
Ludicrous Punishment. In the first volume of the "Library of American Biography, conducted by Jared Sparks," the following incident in the life of Ethan Allen shows the character of the government in Vermont in 1774, when the inhabitants were resisting the claims of New-York to jurisdiction over their territory. A Committee of Safety was the highest judicatory, and Allen was Col. Commandant of the territory. If any person presumed to act under the authority of the State of N. York, he was immediately arraigned and judgement pronounced against him, in the presence of many persons, by which he was sentenced to be tied to a tree and chastised "with the twigs of the wilderness" on his naked back, to the number of two hundred

stripes, and immediately expelled from the district, and threatened with death if he should return, unless specially permitted by the convention.

"In the midst of these signs, the mode of punishment was sometimes rather ludicrous than severe. In the town of Arlington lived a doctor who openly professed himself a partizan of New-York, and was accustomed to speak disrespectfully of the Convention and Committees, espousing the cause of the New-York Claimants, and advising people to purchase lands under their title. He was admonished by his neighbors, and made to understand that this tone of conversation was not acceptable, and was requested to change it, or at least to show his prudence by remaining silent. Far from operating any reform—these hints only stirred up the ire of the courageous doctor, who forthwith armed himself with pistols and other weapons of defence, proclaiming his sentiments more boldly than ever, setting opposition at defiance, and threatening to try the full effects of his personal powers and implements of warfare on any man who should have the temerity to approach him with an unfriendly design. Such a boast was likely to call up the martial spirits of his opponents, who accordingly came upon the doctor at an unguarded moment and obliged him to surrender at discretion. He was then transferred to the Green Mountain Tavern, in Bennington, where he was arraigned before the Committee, who, not satisfied with his defence, sentenced him to a novel punishment, which they ordered to be put in immediate execution.

"Before the door of this tavern, which served the double purpose of a court-house and an inn, stood a sign-post twenty-five feet high, the top of which was adorned with the skin of a Catamount, stuffed to the size of life, with its head turned towards New-York, and its jaws distended, showing large naked teeth, and grinning terror to all who should approach from that quarter. It was the judgment of the court that the contumacious doctor should be tied in a chair and drawn up by a rope to the Catamount, where he was to remain suspended two hours—which punishment was inflicted in the presence of a numerous assemblage of people, much to their satisfaction and merriment. The doctor was then let down and permitted to depart to his own house."

Salem Observer, April 12, 1834.

From the "Essex Register," Feb. 19, 1820.

Burning of a Negro in Georgia.

From the Augusta (Geo.) Chronicle, Feb. 1.

Execution.—On Friday last two negro men, named Ephraim and Sam, were executed in conformity to their sentence for the murder of their master, Mr. Thomas Hancock, of Edgefield District, South Carolina; Sam was burnt, and Ephraim hung, and his head severed from his body and publicly exposed. The circumstances attending the crime for which these miserable beings have suffered, were of a nature so aggravated as imperiously demanded the terrible punishment which has been inflicted upon them.

The burning of malefactors is a punishment only resorted to when absolute necessity demands a signal example. It must be a horrid and appalling sight to see a human being consigned to the flames. Let even Fancy picture the scene,—the pile, the stake, the victim! The mind sickens, and sinks under the oppression of its own feelings. What then must be the dread reality! From some of the spectators we learn that it was a scene which transfixed in breathless horror almost every one who witnessed it. As the flames approached him, the piercing shrieks of the unfortunate victim struck upon the heart with a fearful, painful vibration; but when the devouring element seized upon his body, all was hushed. Yet the cry of agony still thrilled in the ear, and an involuntary and sympathetic shudder ran thro' the crowd. We hope that this awful dispensation of justice may be attended with such salutary effects as to forever preclude the necessity of its repetition. Communication.

If any Massachusetts man can read the above without shuddering, and experiencing alternate emotions of horror and indignation, his heart must be harder than a millstone and colder than the ice of the poles. We know not the particular circumstances of the crime for which this poor wretch suffered, but as far as we can learn from the public prints, it was for the murder of his Master. The probability is there was some provocation; for such dire deeds are not perpetrated without a strong and powerful impulse. It is however of no consequence; no matter what was his crime, such a punishment was abominable, and could not be inflicted, even if the laws permitted it, in our State. If that monster who committed the Stoneham murder in cold blood, impelled solely by avarice, had not put an end to his own life, but had awaited his conviction, had been sentenced to such a punishment, although he would have merited, perhaps more than any other offender who has appeared in our times, the greatest sufferings, yet such a sentence could not be carried into effect. The people would have risen at once, animated by one sentiment, and without the least previous concert have prevented it. Every man in the Commonwealth, waiving all distinctions of condition or age, would have been seen, without consulting his neighbour or considering consequences, putting a new flint in his musket and girding on his sword. Thank God! our feelings and love of order and obedience to proper authority can never be put to such a trial; for the moment we became free, and created our own political institutions, we made it a fundamental article of our Constitution of Government that "no magistrate or court of law shall inflict cruel or unusual punishment." In Georgia such a punishment would not be inflicted upon a white man for any crime; and in the name of Heaven, who deserves the greatest punishment for offences,—the white man, who is instructed in the principles of religion and morality, and is therefore justly accountable for his actions, or the negro, who is kept by the policy of the laws and the power of public opinion in a state of absolute ignorance of his duties, lest he should obtain a knowledge of his rights?   D.

Singular account from the "Salem Gazette," April 13, 1824.

ARREST OF THE DEAD.

The United States Gazette says:—

"While the papers from the south and the west are bringing back to us the report from Mr. Degrand's paper of the attachment of a dead body in Boston, the Eastern papers are bringing us assurances of the total illegality of any such act, and a contradiction of some of the important parts of Mr. Degrand's tale of horror. At the time of the first appearance of this story in our city, a gentleman of information assured the public through the medium of our columns that any such act was unlawful. The Salem Gazette appears to think that no act of the kind was ever lawful in Massachusetts. The Boston Courier states that in Feb., 1812, the legislature of Massachusetts passed a law making it highly penal for any civil officer to take the body of any deceased person, and the writer who furnishes this information says that 'he never heard that any such act of barbarism was ever attempted in that Commonwealth,' but that the law was enacted to guard against the possibility of such an occurrence, by a mistake in the application of the terms, 'we command you to take the body of A.B.' andc.

"This writer undoubtedly knows better than we both the laws and customs of his own state. But we have some recollections of an event of this nature transpiring in the southeastern part of Massachusetts. If we have not forgotten the events (or remembered some that never took place), a Sheriff in Barnstable county, we think in Brewster or Dennis, attached the body of a deceased debtor on its way to the grave, about the year 1811. A circumstance that fixes this event the more firmly in our mind is that it transpired about this season of the year, the time of the gubernatorial election in that State, and was used as a subject of reproach to one of the political parties; and we incline to believe that this act, or, if it never took place, the report of it (for it was talked of), gave rise to the law mentioned in the Courier.

"It is proper, in concluding these remarks, to state that to attach a dead body in Massachusetts is now against the law; and if the act ever took place which is detailed by Mr. Degrand, it was done by the advice of an ignorant attorney."

We are enabled to give an accurate statement of the event to which the editor of the U.S. Gazette above alludes; we copy it from a publication made at the time:—

"On the 20th October, 1811, Capt. Chillingsworth Foster, jun., Æt. about 41 years, departed this life; on the same day Benjamin Bangs, Esq., of

Harwich, with one Mr. Scotto Berry, of the same place, called at the house of the deceased for payment of a sum of about one hundred and thirty dollars, due said Bangs, and requested the father of the deceased to give him his security, said Bangs well knowing the parent to be in low circumstances, and about seventy-five years old, and the mother about the same age. The father refused to comply, stating his inability to answer so great a demand without suffering immediate distress. The said Bangs then declared that if he did not comply, it was in his power to arrest the body of the deceased. The father still refused, and Bangs left the house; and a most distressed one it was, this being the last son out of three, left these aged parents, the other two being lost at sea, or died.

"The Monday following was appointed to have the deceased buried, when Col. Jonathan Snow appeared as Sheriff, with a writ to serve on the body. Here the melancholy scene commenced, a part of the relations being assembled, with the aged parents convulsed in sorrow; no one can paint their feelings but those who have children and are denied them the right of Christian burial. The usual ceremonies on such occasions were however performed, and an appropriate prayer was delivered by the Rev. John Simpkins, and the funeral procession formed and proceeded with the corpse about one and a half mile, and very near to the spot of the grave, when the said Sheriff arrested the coffin, without any service on the body, and it was set down in the middle of the highway nearly abreast of said Bangs' dwelling house, and forbid proceeding any further. A large company who followed, with the mourners, soon after retired, and left the officer in charge of the body. After lying in this situation for some time, one of the Grand Jurors ordered it out of the high road; this was complied with by the Sheriff, by placing it under the window of the said Bangs, and about sunset still further removed it into Bangs' dwelling-house. By this inhuman proceeding the aged parents were deprived of seeing their last and only son buried, as were the widow of the deceased and five children. So distressing a scene never was witnessed in this place, and perhaps not in the most barbarous nations. Between seven and eight of the clock, the same evening, the body was buried by a few individuals, and by the consent of said Benjamin Bangs, Esq., after he had inflicted all the wounds he could on the feelings of the poor grey-headed parents and their relations."

The barbarity and illegality of this conduct of B. Bangs, Esq. (an influential democrat of that day), were viewed with indignation from all quarters. The statute of Feb., 1812, on this subject was not passed to render illegal the arrest of a dead body of a debtor, for that was always illegal, but its object was to fix the punishment, instead of leaving it to the discretion of the Courts. Many undoubtedly recollect the instance at Portland several years before, in which a debtor who was on the limits was suddenly taken sick and carried out of the limits, where he died. It was then decided to be the law that the debtor's bond was not broken unless his body was out of the limits by his own agency and will.

So disinterring dead bodies of men was always a misdemeanor, but in 1815 a law was passed by our General Court to fix the penalties.

The case of Stephen Merrill Clark is remembered by many people in Salem and its vicinity.

Supreme Judicial Court.

At the present term of this Court in Salem, Andrew Dunlap, John Foster, and Solomon Whipple, Esqrs. were admitted Counsellors, and Asa W. Wildes, Esq. an attorney of said Court.

Capital Trial.—On Tuesday Stephen Merrill Clark, a lad about 15 years of age, was indicted for the crime of Arson alleged to have been committed in Newburyport, was arraigned the same day, and pleaded not guilty. The day for his trial is not yet fixed.—The Court assigned him Leverett Saltonstall and John G. King, Esquires, for his counsel on his trial.

Salem Observer, Nov. 4, 1820.

Clark was subsequently convicted of the crime for which he was tried, and executed upon Salem Neck in 1821. He had made a confession of his guilt; but considering his youth, and the circumstances of his having been instigated by others, as was believed, to the commission of the crime, many humane people thought there should have been some mitigation of the punishment.